BROTHERHOOD
OF GOD

A Book of Masonic Prayers

GARRON C. DANIELS

To my darling Nathalia,
who inspired and supported me
in writing this book in hopes
to serve the Brotherhood.

TABLE OF CONTENTS

PREFACE

In my studies of Masonry and short time of work in Ministry, I noticed the alarming lack of prayers within the fraternity. Most of the prayers I found in my research revolved around blessings for food, some memorial/military prayers, very few prayers for a death, and then of course prayers to be said during stated lodge meetings. When looking at these prayers, I thought to myself, "If we are to be Masons in every part of our lives, shouldn't we have prayers to use for every part of our lives?"

In my faith tradition as an Episcopalian, our *Book of Common Prayer* (1979) has a number of prayers to be used in any given situation. I thought it best to have something similar to that, but for Freemasons! My hope is that this small book will help guide you in both your spiritual and Masonic journey in life. This book is not just for Chaplains to use; though I would love for all Masonic Chaplains to use it and bring it to their lodges. Rather, this is for every Mason who is in need of prayer for any given situation. I hope you use it and find it fulfilling to your everyday needs.

So may this book serve you in your joy, stress, sorrow, and celebration. No matter what, let the Supreme Architect speak to you through these prayers in order to assist you in whatever need you may have. Remember that no matter what, rely on your fellow man and above all, your God.

Garron C. Daniels
The Feast of Saint Joseph, 2022

PRAYERS FOR
THE WORLD

For Brothers around the World

Supreme Architect of the Universe, who has graciously guided us in our own nation: We humbly ask that you guide our brothers around the world; that they may meet and work for the betterment of their fellow man and for the betterment of their Masonic journey. We especially pray that they find the means to spread the light of Masonry not only in their own lives, but across the world. In this we pray. Amen.

FOR PEACE

Supreme Architect of the Universe, direct our world in order to fulfill the full image of your perfect design. By doing so, may we find not violence, but peace and love amongst us all. May we come together in tranquility and in harmony under your mighty hand. In your most magnifying and holy name we pray. Amen.

For Peace Amongst the Nations

God of Mercy, guide the nations and the brothers who represent them to find justice, truth, and peace in order to come together to build your Kingdom. For we know we cannot do this if we are divided. Guide and restore us, Almighty Father. Amen.

FOR PEACE AMONGST INTERNATIONAL BROTHERS, LODGES, AND JURISDICTIONS

Supreme Architect of the Universe, we ask you for guidance, patience, and reconciliation amongst our brethren. We know that we have strayed from the mission and brotherly love that are due to one another. May we find peace and charity once more in order to strive for a more perfect future, together, in unity. We pray this in your most Holy name. Amen.

FOR OUR ENEMIES AND THOSE WHO WISH TO DO US HARM

Almighty God, who calls us to love our enemies, deliver us and those who wish to do us harm from all evil, hatred, cruelty, dark thoughts, and revenge. May we reconcile with one another under your loving embrace. In your holy name we pray. Amen.

Prayers for our Nation

FOR OUR COUNTRY

Supreme Architect of the Universe, who has guided those who have built this nation: Guide us, too, so that we may do your will and create a nation built on charity, brotherhood, freedom, and hope. Help defend our liberties and assist in our daily endeavors to seek justice and truth for all people. Let your spirit fill us with wisdom to protect and sustain the land that you have given us and may our hearts and minds forever show our thankfulness. In your most holy name we pray. Amen.

For the President of the United States and all in Governmental Authority

Almighty God, who governs and reigns supreme above all; grant that the President of the United States

_____ (insert name),

the Governor of this State _____ (insert name), and all in authority, the wisdom and strength do your will and serve your people. Fill their hearts and minds with truth and righteousness so that they may do your will. Protect and sustain them in all their work and guide them out of the fear and darkness they may face. In your righteous name we pray. Amen.

FOR CONGRESS OR A STATE LEGISLATURE

Almighty Creator, who established order in the chaos: We ask you to guide our Senators and Representatives in Congress (or in the State Legislature) that they may enact laws that fulfill your mission. May they be guided by truth, morality, and justice as you have defined in your own mighty laws. In your holy name we pray. Amen.

FOR COURTS OF JUSTICE

Almighty God, who sends judgment to all: We ask that you guide the courts of justice and those who work within them. May they be led by your wisdom and righteousness. Help them to discern the truth and administer impartial justice to all that come before them. In your Holy Name we pray. Amen.

FOR THE GOVERNMENT

Supreme Architect of the Universe, who calls for unity of all: Grant that all branches of our government may work as one unified structure in order to bring peace, safety, justice, and truth to all your people. Grant that also the citizens within this government may work together in order to elect and work with the leaders of this nation to gain that unity. In your Holy Name we pray. Amen.

FOR LOCAL GOVERNMENT

Almighty God, guide those of this local government of the County of _____ (insert name) and City of _____ that those elected may lead with justice, truth, and tranquility in mind. May they faithfully serve their office and help guide your people into peace and prosperity. In this we pray. Amen.

FOR AN ELECTION

Heavenly Father, most powerful above all: Guide your people in the election of their officials and representatives so that they may elect leaders who continue to strive for the mission of your heavenly kingdom and help restore balance in the nation. In this we pray. Amen.

For those in the Armed Forces of Our Country

Almighty God, we ask that you care and protect all our armed forces at home and abroad. Especially care for our brothers who are amongst them. Give them the clarity of mind and the strength to face the dangers and challenges that are to come. May you protect and hold them close, Lord. In your most mighty and powerful name we pray. Amen.

PRAYERS FOR GENERAL USE

FOR TIMES OF CONFLICT

Oh God of Peace, help guide us in the midst of the chaos, uncertainty, and conflict that has arisen. Help guide us in order to forgive one another for their transgressions and enact reconciliation in order to find peace amongst us. In your Holy Name we pray. Amen.

FOR FIRST RESPONDERS

Almighty Architect, assist our first responders in their pursuit to care and protect those in need. Protect them from the dangers they face and the evil they must confront. Help them show compassion, love, and kindness to all they work with, in hopes that they may receive the same. Guide them in their responsibility to bring order within the chaos. In your most powerful Name we pray. Amen.

FOR THE WORKER

Almighty Father, who sees the works of your creation: Guide our fellow workers in their endeavors so that they may produce work that strengthens our society. Help them provide for their family and fellow workers. Assist them also in finding rest from their work, as you also found rest on the seventh day of creation. In this we pray. Amen.

FOR THE NEWLY RETIRED

Supreme Architect and Builder of this World: Guide our brother as he steps into a new chapter of his life. Help him seek a new purpose in life filled with joy, rest, and forever seeking deeper knowledge of you. Help him in all the transitions that are to take place and assist him in the joys and challenges that are to come his way. In your Holy Name we pray. Amen.

FOR THE UNEMPLOYED

Almighty God, we recognize the difficulties that are created from the lack of work. Guide your people so that they may find purpose and fulfillment of their duties here on earth. Guide them so that they may receive fair wages in all their endeavors. In your Holy Name we pray. Amen.

For the Poor

Lord God, we know that the poor will always be amongst us: Grant that with your help and guidance we may assist the poor in gaining shelter, food, and security. Fill our hearts with warmth and charity to share in abundance to our brothers and sisters who need it most. In this we pray. Amen.

FOR THE OPPRESSED

Lord God, we ask for mercy and protection to all those who face oppression in the forms of injustice, discrimination, terror, disease, and death. We especially pray for all our brothers and sisters in all Masonic Organizations that may face similar challenges and forms of oppression. Show them your love and compassion so that they may be strengthened in the face of their difficulties. Help them in eliminating the evil and cruelty they face and restore equality and unity amongst us all. In this we pray. Amen.

FOR THE PRISONERS

Heavenly Father, who sees and hears all those that face imprisonment: Grant all prisoners peace and love amongst them. Help guide them in the way of justice and truth. Help those that are guilty to repent and turn towards you and your loving grace. If they are innocent yet imprisoned, guide them to seek justice in order to be released from their shackles. Guide also our brothers who have found themselves imprisoned. Help them seek light in you and turn away from their errors. In your Holy Name we pray. Amen.

FOR AGRICULTURE

Almighty Creator, who makes the earth fruitful and abundant with life: Bless your lands so that they may produce a bountiful harvest in order to feed and nourish your people. Give us the weather needed in order to plant and reap these benefits during harvest. Guide also those that work in your fields. Keep them safe in their work as they provide for your people. In this we pray. Amen.

FOR STUDENTS OF ALL STUDIES

God of Ultimate Wisdom, guide the students of (insert school, college, university) so that they may find new discoveries and increase their knowledge of your creation. Help them as they pursue their studies and assist in their continuous learning so that they may pursue knowledge and truth for the rest of their days. In your glorious Name we pray. Amen.

Prayers for Personal and Family Life

FOR THE MORNINGS

Almighty Father, as a new day begins, may I be renewed by your strength and wisdom to serve you and the Fraternity in all that I do. May you be in my mind and heart throughout the day, remembering to give you praise for my successes and ask for your assistance in my challenges. In your Most Glorious Name I pray. Amen.

FOR THE END OF THE DAY

Supreme Architect of the Universe, Governor of Night and Day: I thank you for the blessings that I have received and the assistance in my challenges. As the world turns to the quiet of night, may my mind and heart find rest and relaxation in your calming embrace. May also I be protected tonight from all harm and danger that I may face in order to awake the next day to serve you and the Fraternity in all that I do. In your Holy Name I pray. Amen.

FOR FAMILIES

Almighty Father, who brought creation together into an unbreakable bond: Guide the members of our families and those in our homes. Help assist in putting all evil, anger, jealousy, pride, and bitterness away from our lives. Guide us towards understanding, patience, love, compassion, kindness, unity, and knowledge of you. Turn hearts and minds towards you in remembrance of the bond that we all share. In this we pray. Amen.

FOR OUR MASONIC FAMILY

Supreme Architect of Universe, who creates everlasting bonds in life: Help in guiding the brothers I call a part of my Masonic Family, in order to find compassion, friendship, charity, and brotherly love amongst us. Remind us in our hearts and minds that we have come together in order to seek your Holy Light and let no evil and or darkness separate us from that love and friendship you have offered. In this we pray. Amen.

FOR NEWLY ENGAGED

Almighty Father, we ask for your presence and blessing upon our newly engaged brother and his intended. May you strengthen their bond and guide them as they prepare to spend their lives together. Be ever present with them in this new journey. In your Holy Name we pray. Amen.

FOR NEWLY MARRIED

Almighty Creator, who saw creation alone and saw fit to bring it a spouse: Guide our newly married brother so that he and his spouse may know the unity and love that you have shared with creation. May they continue this journey of life together and bless them in all their endeavors. Be present in both their joys and sorrows and help lift them closer to you and your everlasting Kingdom. In your most Holy and Loving Name we pray. Amen.

FOR EXPECTING COUPLE

Almighty Father, bringer of life: Guide our brother
_____ (insert name) and his spouse
_____ as they prepare for the journey of parenthood.
Bless them as they endure the pregnancy with all its joys and
hardships. Assist in their mental and physical preparation as they
prepare to welcome new life into your world. In this we pray.
Amen.

For a Safe Delivery

Most Merciful God, we thank you for assisting our brother and his spouse as they endured the pain and anxiety of childbirth. We thank you for the blessing of a new life in this world and the doctors and nurses who helped bring the child safely here. We ask that you continue to guide this new family and the life they will share together. In your Holy Name we pray. Amen.

FOR PARENTS

Heavenly Father, giver of life and creator of all: Guide our brother
_____ (insert name) and his spouse
_____ in their newfound journey of parenthood.
Guide them in order to find charity, love, clarity, and calmness in
all the days of their lives. Help lift them out of the difficulties and
hardships they face and see that they work together to strive for a
life built on the solid foundation of you and your mighty Word.
In this we pray. Amen.

FOR GRANDPARENTS AND OTHER RELATIVES

Almighty Creator, who creates the bonds between all of our family: Guide our brother who is the _____ (insert relation to child) of _____ (insert name of child). Help him care, protect, and love him/her. Help him in building up the lives of the child and his/her parents as they grow and change together. In your Holy Name we pray. Amen.

FOR AN ADOPTED CHILD

Supreme Architect of the Universe, who creates the bonds of family not only by blood, but by your mighty force: Guide the new parents of _____ (insert name of child). Bless them with the love, care, and compassion they need to care for this new addition to their family. Assist them in creating an inseparable bond. May they be united for the rest of their days. In your Name we pray. Amen.

FOR CHILDREN

Almighty Father, who takes joy in the new life of your creation: Bless the children and those that care for them so they may grow in the knowledge and love of you. May they grow to understand love, joy, and the true good of this world. Protect them from the evil of this world and those who would do them harm. May they forever and always be loved and blessed by your mighty hand. In this we pray. Amen.

FOR YOUNG PERSONS GROWING UP

Supreme Architect, as we grow in the love and care you have given us, also help our children who are growing up amongst your creation. As they grow older, the world around them will change and at times seem unfamiliar to them. Help them to better understand your ways and find you in their journey of life. Protect them in all their endeavors and changes they face. Assist them in recognizing right from wrong and may they be guided by your light out of the darkness. In this we ask and pray. Amen.

FOR THE AGED

Most Ancient and wise Master of the Universe, look with tenderness and mercy upon all those progressing in their years of life. Assist them in their weakness, distress, isolation, confusion, frustration, or any other challenges they may face. Provide them an understanding of their place in this world and the glorious purpose they serve in providing for your Heavenly Kingdom. May you guide them in their endeavors and all those that wish to help care for them. Increase their love and compassion for the world. In your Holy Name we pray. Amen.

For those in Isolation or Alone

Supreme Architect, who sees all creation in time and space: Grant companionship and comfort to all those who live alone or are in a time of isolation. Assist in connecting them with their community, whether it be their fellow brothers or the community at large. May they find comfort in knowing that they have a network of those who think of them, pray for them, and care about them. Give them strength in this time, now and always. In this we pray. Amen.

FOR THOSE WHO ARE ABSENT

Almighty Creator, who stretches his mighty hands across the Universe: Help in connecting us with those who are absent from us. Though we may be physically apart, remind us that our connection remains deeper than we could possibly comprehend. Be with us as we draw nearer to one another and assist in reconnecting us once more. In your most Glorious Name we pray. Amen.

FOR TRAVELERS

Great Architect of Heaven and Earth, who is ever present with us no matter where we go: Guide those who are traveling, especially (insert particular place/destination). Protect them on their journey for any dangers that they may face and bring them safely back home at the end of their new adventure. In your Holy Name we pray and ask for this. Amen.

FOR A BIRTHDAY

O God, who celebrates the continuation of creation each day: Bless our brother _____ (insert name) as he begins another year of life with us all. Grant that he may continue to grow in kindness, wisdom, grace, and charity for the rest of his days. In your most Magnificent Name we pray. Amen.

ANOTHER PRAYER FOR A BIRTHDAY

O Heavenly Father, what joy we have gained from our brother _____ (insert name) this year. Grant that we may spend the coming year with him as he grows as a man, a Mason, and as a servant to your Heavenly Kingdom. Protect and guide him all the rest of his days. In this we pray. Amen.

FOR THOSE WE LOVE

Almighty Creator, who opens the hearts of all: Guide those that we have placed close to hearts in love and care. May they be protected by your mighty hand. May we also continue to grow in our love not only for those close to us, but for all of your creation, especially our fellow man. In this we ask and pray for your most excellent guidance. Amen.

FOR VICTIMS OF ADDICTION

O God of Truth and Hope: Look with tenderness and compassion upon all those who face the destruction of addiction. Restore their health and freedom once more. Break the chains that bind them and set them toward a path of redemption and renewal. Strengthen them when they feel like falling back into darkness and show them mercy on their lifelong road to recovery. Now and forevermore we pray. Amen.

FOR GUIDANCE

Supreme Architect of the Universe, shepherd and guide of all your people: Lead us in all our work and doings, that we may forever strive towards your will and put forward the mission of your Kingdom above all else. In this we pray. Amen.

ANOTHER PRAYER FOR GUIDANCE

O Supreme Architect, Master and Creator of all, we are but lost sheep in the darkness. Without your presence we are utterly alone. Guide and protect us so that we may come in unity to strive towards your light in order to create a world more fitting to your purpose. Give us the grace and wisdom to steer through all the uncertainties we face and help relieve us from our worries and constraints. Forever be at our side, to comfort and guide us. In this we pray to you. Amen.

FOR STRENGTH

Supreme Architect, God of power and might: Help us in our times of weakness and uncertainty. Give us the strength we need in order to do your work. Lift us up with confidence and determination in order to serve you and your Heavenly Kingdom for the rest of our days. In your Holy Name we pray. Amen.

FOR PROTECTION

Heavenly Father, who shines light into the darkness: Guard us against all the challenges, struggles, and evil we may face. Protect us, your mortal servants, that we may continue our journey towards your mighty salvation. In your Most Holy Name we pray. Amen.

FOR DEDICATION TO GOD

O Most Merciful God, Father of mercy: I have fallen away from your love and grace. I have forgotten the light and have chosen darkness over your beauty and glory. I have led with anger and selfishness in my life and have chosen a path not fitting for a Mason. Hear my plea so that I may dedicate myself to you once again and be filled with the knowledge and love of you. Help me see and hear you once more. Restore in me a clean heart O God so that I may serve you for the rest of my days. In this I pray to you. Amen.

PRAYERS FOR GENERAL MASONIC USE

MEAL BLESSING

Supreme Architect of the Universe, we thank you for the brethren present and the fellowship we are about to take part in. We ask that you bless our meal so that it may nourish our bodies and give us the energy needed to do your work. In your Holy Name we pray. Amen.

ANOTHER MEAL BLESSING

Almighty Father, source of all bounties and harvest: Bless the meal that lays before us and those who helped prepare it. May it bring us a new sense of strength and energy so that we may go forth in serving you forevermore. In this we pray. Amen.

ANOTHER MEAL BLESSING

God of Creation, who is the ultimate source of nourishment: Bless the food and the brethren present here today. May we eat and commune in your holy presence. May we move forward here today in peace and harmony, forever praising and recognizing your glorious works. In your Holy Name we pray. Amen.

FOR SOCIAL GATHERINGS

Grand Master of Universe, who governs over all creation: We thank you for allowing friends and brethren alike to come together in unity and harmony. We thank you for this opportunity to build our community and brotherhood outside of Lodge, always remembering the importance of both labor and refreshment. Grant that our time together may endue your servants with a sense of enthusiasm and new found energy to serve the Brotherhood and your Holy Kingdom. In this we pray. Amen.

Another Prayer for Social Gatherings

Supreme Architect, we thank you for this opportunity of brotherhood and fellowship here today. We thank you for the opportunity for us to build up the Fraternity in ways that go beyond the walls of Lodge. We praise you for this time together and ask that you bless all the friends and brethren here as we move forward forever singing and praising your Holy Name. In this we pray. Amen.

ANOTHER PRAYER FOR SOCIAL GATHERINGS

Almighty Father, we thank you for this opportunity of refreshment and brotherly love and all that you have continued to do for us. We thank you for the blessing that is Masonry and the brotherhood as a whole. Grant us strength and a new sense of energy that will allow us to continue the mission of Freemasonry and continue to serve you and your Heavenly Kingdom. In your Holy Name we pray. Amen.

FOR CHARITABLE EVENTS

Grand Architect of the World, giver of all good things: Grant that our charitable cause of _____ (insert name of event or organization) may prosper today so as to help those most in need. Bless this event and the brethren who are assisting it. May we work to help provide for your people by our love and charity in the work that we are called to do. In your Holy Name we pray. Amen.

FOR NEW LEADERSHIP

Grant Master of the Universe, governor of all: Bless the new officers and leaders of _____ (insert Lodge name). May they be guided by the principals of your Holy Word and that of the tenets and teachings of Freemasonry. May you strengthen them in all their endeavors. Create in them a new sense of energy and passion for the Craft so that the Lodge and your Heavenly Kingdom may prosper. In your Name we pray. Amen.

FOR DIFFICULT TIMES

Most Merciful God, who sees all the struggles of your humble servants: Guide us through the struggles we face as a Lodge. We have hit a time of uncertainty, loss, and pain. We do not know what our future holds, but we do know of the great comfort you provide for us through the darkness. Give us the strength, knowledge, and determination to walk towards the light in all that we do. May we prosper once again, forever praising you for the assistance you have given us. In this we pray. Amen.

FOR A PROSPECTIVE MEMBER

Almighty Father, author of wisdom and truth: Guide our prospective member, _____ (insert name), as he discerns whether to join Freemasonry. May he be guided by your mighty hand as he seeks deeper understanding and knowledge of Masonry and the light it has to offer. In your Holy Name we pray. Amen.

FOR A DEDICATION/RE-DEDICATION

Supreme Architect of the Universe, we thank you for the prosperity and strength you have given our Fraternity over the years. As we come together to dedicate (or re-dedicate) this building to your work through Masonry, we also come to dedicate (or re-dedicate) our lives and works to you, our most esteemed Grand Master of all. May this building and the lives of all the brethren here present help serve you and your Heavenly Kingdom for the rest of our days. In your Most Holy Name we pray. Amen.

FOR LODGE COMMITTEE MEETINGS

Grand Master of the Universe, governor of all creation: Grant that the brothers gathered here today may be led with your wisdom, knowledge, and truth so that we may work to better your Fraternity and live into your Holy Word. May we find clarity of mind and a renewed sense of energy in order to complete the mission of this committee. In your Holy Name we pray. Amen.

FOR THE REFORMATION OF A BROTHER

Supreme Architect of the Universe, shepherd of lost souls: Bless and guide our brother _____(insert name), who has returned to us in search of light. Help in restoring in him a sense of passion and love for the Craft and your Holy Word. Assist in strengthening him in the challenges he may face. Help also the brethren of this Lodge in welcoming him with open arms, just like you welcome all those who love you and return to you. In your Holy Name we pray. Amen.

FOR MASONIC STUDY

Grand Master of the Universe, fountain of wisdom: Grant us clarity of mind and a willingness to learn so that we may gain new knowledge of the Craft and your Holy Word. May we come away from this time of study with a deeper understanding of what it means to be both a Mason and a Man of God. In your Holy Name we pray. Amen.

FOR CELEBRATION OF VETERAN MASONS

Heavenly Father, we come before you today in celebration of our veteran brethren. They fought to protect and defend their nation and the ideals it stands for. So may you also continue to defend and protect them in their own lives; bringing them only peace and comfort the rest of their days. In your Holy Name we pray. Amen.

FOR CELEBRATION OF 50 OR 75 YEARS

Grand Master of the Universe, we gather here today to celebrate the work and life of _____ (insert name). Today we celebrate 50 [or 75] glorious years of his service to the Fraternity and your Holy Kingdom. We ask that you continue to bless our brother with abundance of brotherly love and life so that he may continue to serve the Fraternity and your Holy Word. In this we pray. Amen.

PRAYERS FOR THE SICK AND DYING

FOR A SICK BROTHER

Merciful Father, our one true help and redeemer: We humbly ask for healing and relief of your ill servant, _____ (insert name). Look upon him with your love and mercy. Help him persevere against the illness and all other afflictions he may face. Restore in him good health and praise of you and your miraculous works. In your Most Holy Name we pray. Amen.

PRAYER A SICK BROTHER CAN SAY

Merciful Father, my one true help and redeemer: I humbly ask for healing and relief from my sickness. Look upon me with your love and mercy. Help me persevere against the illness and all other afflictions that I may face. Restore in me good health and praise of you and your miraculous works. In your Most Holy Name I pray. Amen.

FOR AN OPERATION

Heavenly Father, we ask that you comfort our brother, _____ (insert name), as he prepares for his coming operation. Help him in any suffering and pain that he may face. Fill him with your quiet confidence and love so that he may face his fears and challenges head on; knowing that you are there with him. May he put his hope and trust in you as he faces this challenge and also during his road to recovery. In this we pray. Amen.

PRAYER A BROTHER FACING AN OPERATION CAN SAY

Heavenly Father, I ask that you comfort me for my upcoming operation. Help me in the suffering and pain that I am facing. Fill me with your quiet confidence and love so that I may face my fears and challenges head on; knowing that you are there with me. May I remember to put my hope and trust in you as I face this challenge and the road to recovery afterwards. In this I pray. Amen.

FOR THOSE FACING MENTAL DISTRESS

Father of Mercy, you see your servants in all their darkest times and in the struggles they face. Help our brothers who are facing mental distress. Show them love and kindness in the face of sorrow and fear. Give them strength when they feel weak. Give them comfort when they feel alone. Help them in knowing that you are with them, always and forever. In your Holy Name we pray. Amen.

Thanksgiving for Recovery

Supreme Architect, we rejoice in your great mercy and love for restoring our brother _____ (insert name) back to good health. We thank you for your mighty works in his life and ask that you continue to bless him as he gains back his strength and independence. May we forever remember the healing work of your mighty hands. In your Holy Name we pray. Amen.

A Prayer for the Recovering to say

Supreme Architect, I rejoice in your great mercy and love for restoring me back to good health. I thank you for your mighty works in my life and ask that you continue to bless me as I gain back my strength and independence. May I forever remember the healing work of your mighty hands and know that it was you who helped me during my afflictions. In your Holy Name I forever pray. Amen.

FOR A DYING BROTHER

Supreme Architect of the Universe, giver of life eternal: Look down on your servant _____(insert name of brother) with compassion and grace. Guide him as he approaches the end of his journey here in this mortal world. Take away his pain, fear, and anxieties. Restore in him a heart of love and readiness for you and your life everlasting. Ready also the hearts of his family, friends, and loved ones as they prepare to send him home to his Almighty Father. In your most Holy Name we pray. Amen.

ANOTHER PRAYER FOR A DYING BROTHER

Supreme Architect of the Universe, giver of life eternal: Guide our brother, _____ (insert name), as he enters your celestial lodge above. May he be released from his mortal flesh and the pain and worries of this world. May he be welcomed into your holy embrace. At this time, we also remember that we, too, are mortal and will die one day, and ask that you guide us the rest of our days until we, too, must lay down our working tools. In your Holy Name we pray mercifully. Amen.

FOR A DYING BROTHER TO SAY

Grand Master of the Universe, giver of life eternal: Grant me peace and comfort as I prepare to lay down my working tools of this world so as to enter your celestial lodge. My time has come to an end and I have done as much as I could in your Holy Name and the work of the Fraternity. Help clear my mind of all my worries and uncertainties so that I may prepare to meet you face to face. In this I humbly pray as your loyal and loving servant. Amen.

At the Time/Knowing of Death

Supreme Architect of the Universe, we come before you in mourning for our brother _____ (insert name) who has laid down his working tools to enter into your celestial lodge above. Grant him joy and peace, forever singing your praises in your Heavenly Kingdom. We also ask that you guide his friends, brethren, and loved ones as they both mourn his passing and remember the legacy he has left behind. May we all find peace in knowing we will reunite with him once more. In your Holy Name we pray. Amen.

FOR A SOLDIER KILLED IN THE LINE OF DUTY

Merciful Father, look upon your servants, lying in great agony and sorrow as we mourn the loss of our brother _____ (insert name). He sacrificed his life for his Country and the ideals it stands for. Guide him into your Heavenly Kingdom where he may meet you face to face in awe and love. Guide us all as we remember his life and heroic service to his Country, Fraternity, and your Holy Word. In this we pray. Amen.

For a First Responder Killed in the Line of Duty

Merciful Father, look upon your servants, lying in great agony and sorrow as we mourn the loss of our brother, _____. He sacrificed his life caring for his community and those that he loved. Guide him into your Heavenly Kingdom where he may meet you face to face in awe and love. Guide us all as we remember his life and heroic service to his Community, the Fraternity, and your Holy Word. In this we pray. Amen.

FOR REMEMBRANCE OF OUR MORTALITY

Grand Master of the Universe, creator of all: Guide us in remembering that we are all dust and that to dust we will once again return. Help us in remembering that we are mortal beings who will one day lay down our working tools and join you in your celestial lodge above. May we also remember to live our lives according to your Word, for the betterment of the Fraternity and your Holy Kingdom. Now and forevermore we pray. Amen.

Masonic Bible
Presentation

Brother, you have served your full apprenticeship as a hewer of stone in stone quarries and a bearer of loads. You have sojourned and risen to the noble position of a Master Mason which makes you an overseer of work. You are now a Master Mason that is free to travel to other countries, work and receive the wages of a Master.

You have been given all the tools that you need, and you have been taught their uses. You have been taught how to use the 24-inch gauge to divide your time appropriately. This will help you have 8 hours to rest and 8 hours for the service of your fellow man and the worship of your Creator.

The common gavel has been given to you to rid your conscience and your mind of all superfluities and vices of life. This will help you stand in your proper place in the eternal Heavens and not in a house made with hands when the time comes.

The plumb has been given to you to teach you how to square your actions by the square of virtue and how you can meet and work on the level. The trowel has been given to you to spread brotherly affection and love that binds the Freemason fraternity together. This love cements us together and makes us a Brotherhood that is known worldwide.

But there is something else that you need. Something that all workmen need. You have not yet been given your set of plans.

You have not been given your Trestle Board. It is a privilege and honor to present this Trestle Board to you.

This is the Masonic Bible on which your hands were placed and which you kissed when you were taking your three Masonic obligations at this Masonic altar.

This Bible is your book of plans. It is the most complete set of plans that can be given to any man. This Bible contains plans to sustain you, guide you and comfort you in all weather, in sorrow, in joy, in sickness, in health, in riches, and in poverty. You will find all the answers that you need in this Bible.

You can use this Bible anyhow you want to. We are not the ones to tell you how to use it. You must find out how to use it yourself. You might decide to find light in the ten commandments handed to Moses or the acts of the apostle, or the words of King Solomon or the records in the book of Exodus or the wisdom that comes from the proverbs of King Solomon.

You might find the answers you seek in the words of that humble carpenter who lived a perfect and humble life 2000 years ago. No matter what you decide, turn to this great book for help, and you will find your plan. You may fail this book, but the book will never fail you.

We hereby present to you this Trestle Board, this Book of plans with great blessings and wishes. This Trestle Board is yours to guide and serve you in your business, social and family life.

Now that you have been fully equipped with your Trestle Board, we implore you to go forth and do your work as a Master Mason and a Man.

Note: **This is a Bible presentation ceremony, but you can replace it with any Holy book from another religion.**

Masonic Bible presentation ceremony. Bricks Masons. (2019, January 11). Retrieved April 13, 2022, from https://bricksmasons.com/blogs/masonic-education/masonic-bible-presentation-ceremony

A Note to the Reader

Thank you for purchasing and reading my book! I hope that this book has inspired you and has become a valuable addition to your Masonic library. If you have enjoyed this book, please consider leaving an honest review on your favorite online bookstore website.

As a special thank you for reading this book, please head to www.perfectashlarpublishing.com to access free content and to stay up-to-date with our latest news.

ABOUT THE AUTHOR

Garron C. Daniels is a Freemason from the State of Missouri. He's a member of Brotherhood Lodge #269 in St Joseph, Mo, a member of the Scottish Rite and York Rite, and several other fundraising bodies of Freemasonry. He gains his influence in writing from his studies about the Fraternity as well as his studies in becoming an Episcopal Priest at the University of the South: School of Theology. He continues to dedicate his time in exploring the religious aspects of Masonry and where Christianity plays a role in it.

Check out these Masonic books from Perfect Ashlar Publishing

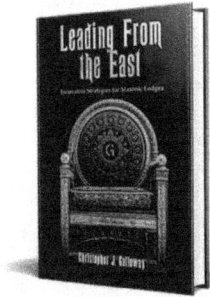

Leading from the East: Innovative Strategies for Masonic Lodges
By Christophor Galloway, PM

Light Reflections: Philosophical Thoughts and Observations of a Texas Freemason
By Bradley E. Kohanke, PM

The Profound Pontifications of Big John Deacon, Freemason Extraordinaire

Volume I – IV

By James "Chris" Williams IV, PM